About *Love Letters: The Coloring Book*

The *Love Letters* series is an alphabet made out of things that I love: leaves, flowers, insects, and other little natural wonders.

Some of the letters are alliterative, such as M for millipede and maple leaf. Other letters represent the names of important people in my life and are made out of their favorite things, or things that in some way represent my relationship with that person.

 If you'd like to know more about why each letter is the way it is and the stories behind the drawings, pick up a copy of the full *Love Letters* book.

This coloring book was a stretch goal reached by my Kickstarter campaign in November 2015. I didn't really believe it would happen, but found the support and interest in my work was much greater than I had anticipated. You are holding this book thanks to the support of my fans and patrons. Their enthusiasm for this project is humbling and I am honored by them.

Consider this book an invitation to collaborate. Feel free to share your coloring pages, and any Love Letters of your own, with me at rheaewing@gmail.com or on twitter @finecomic.

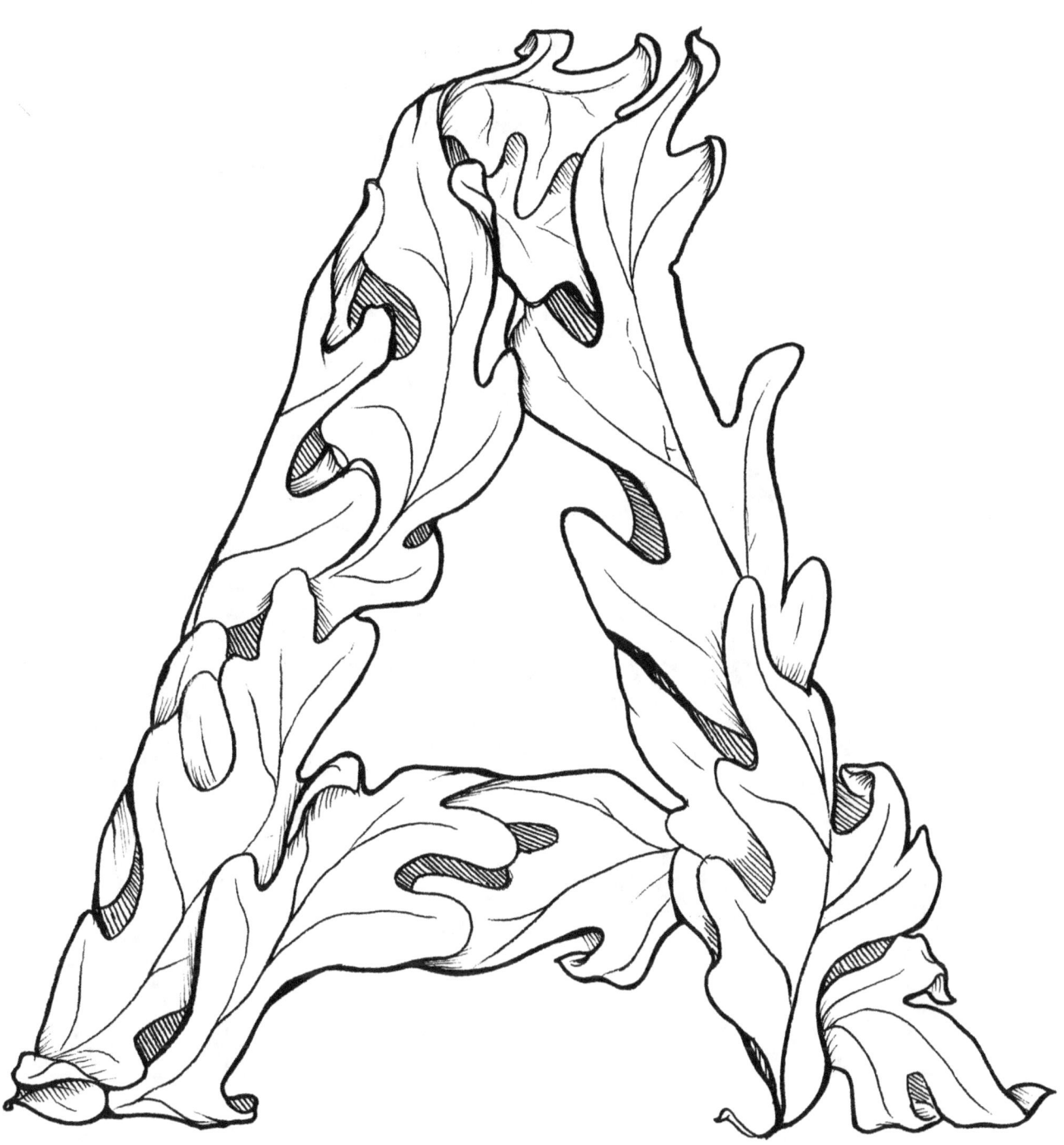

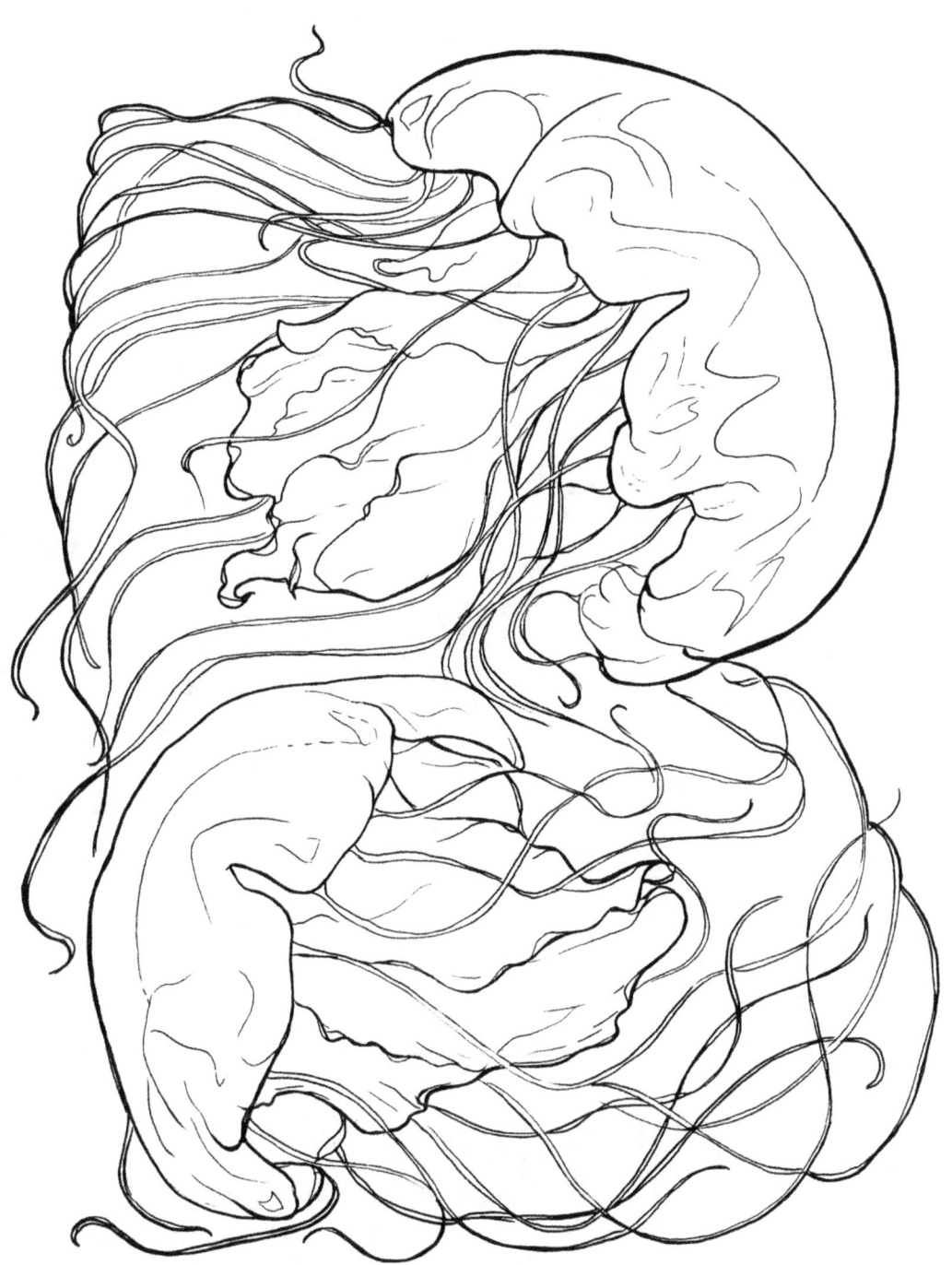

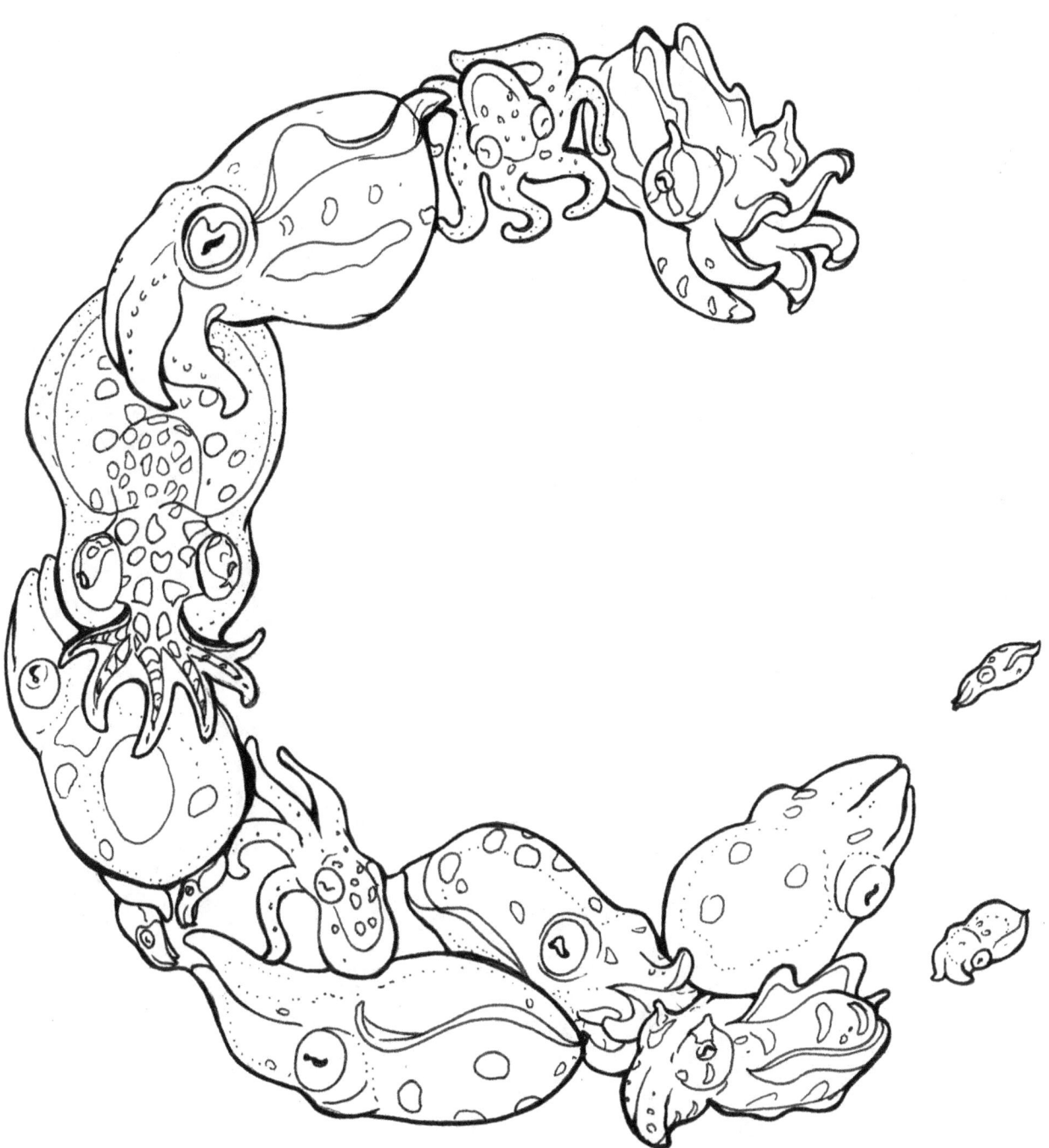

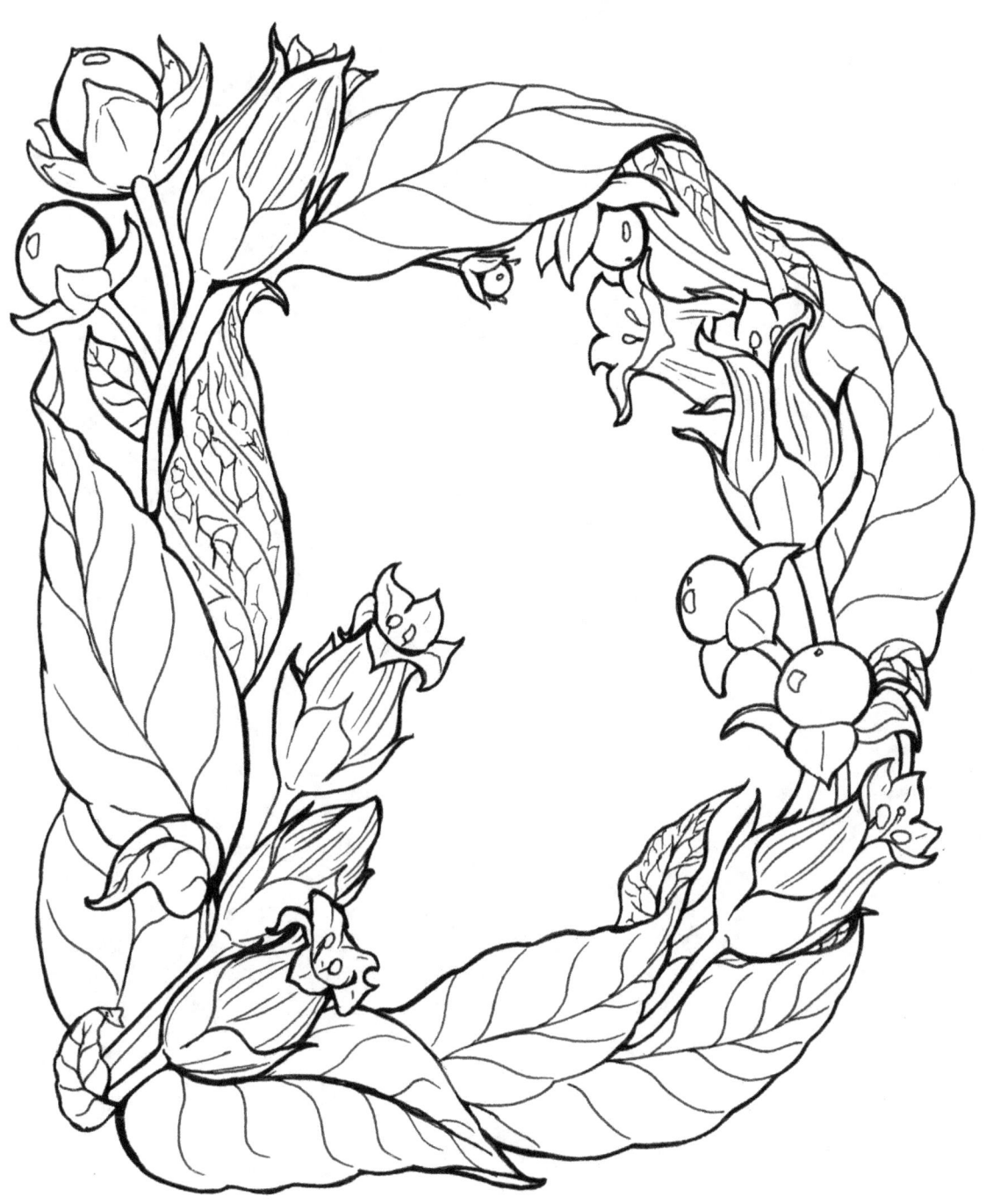

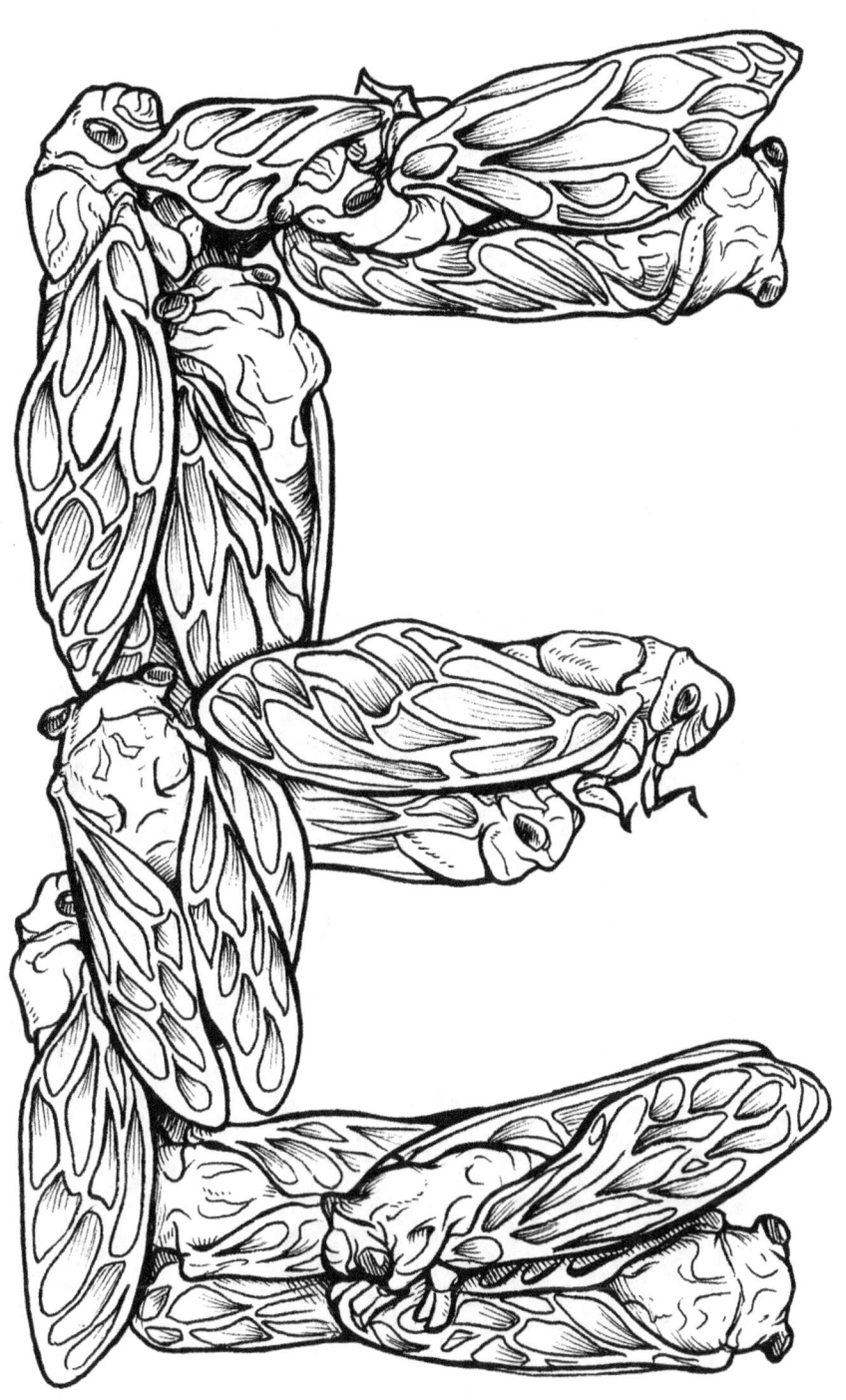

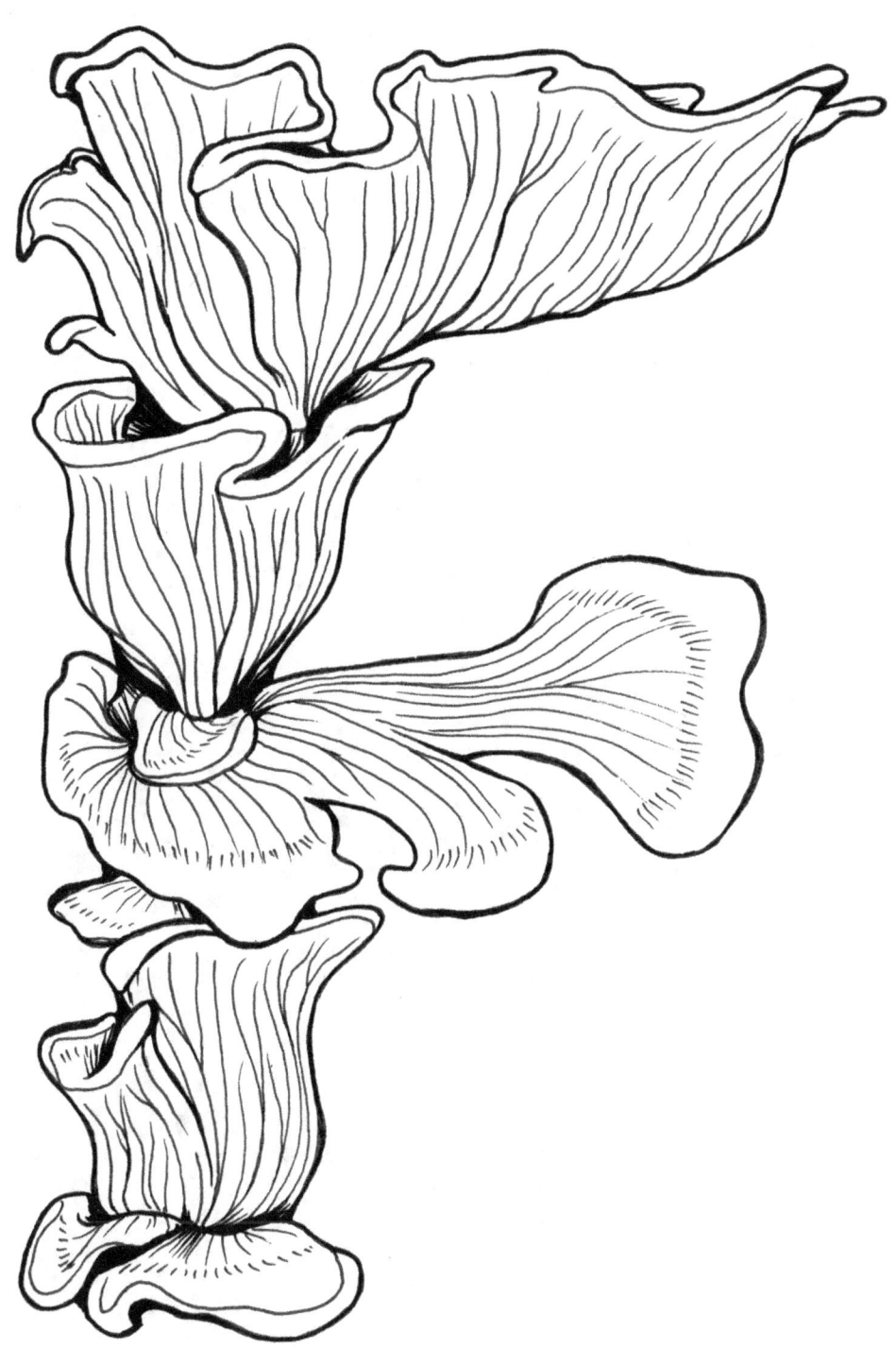

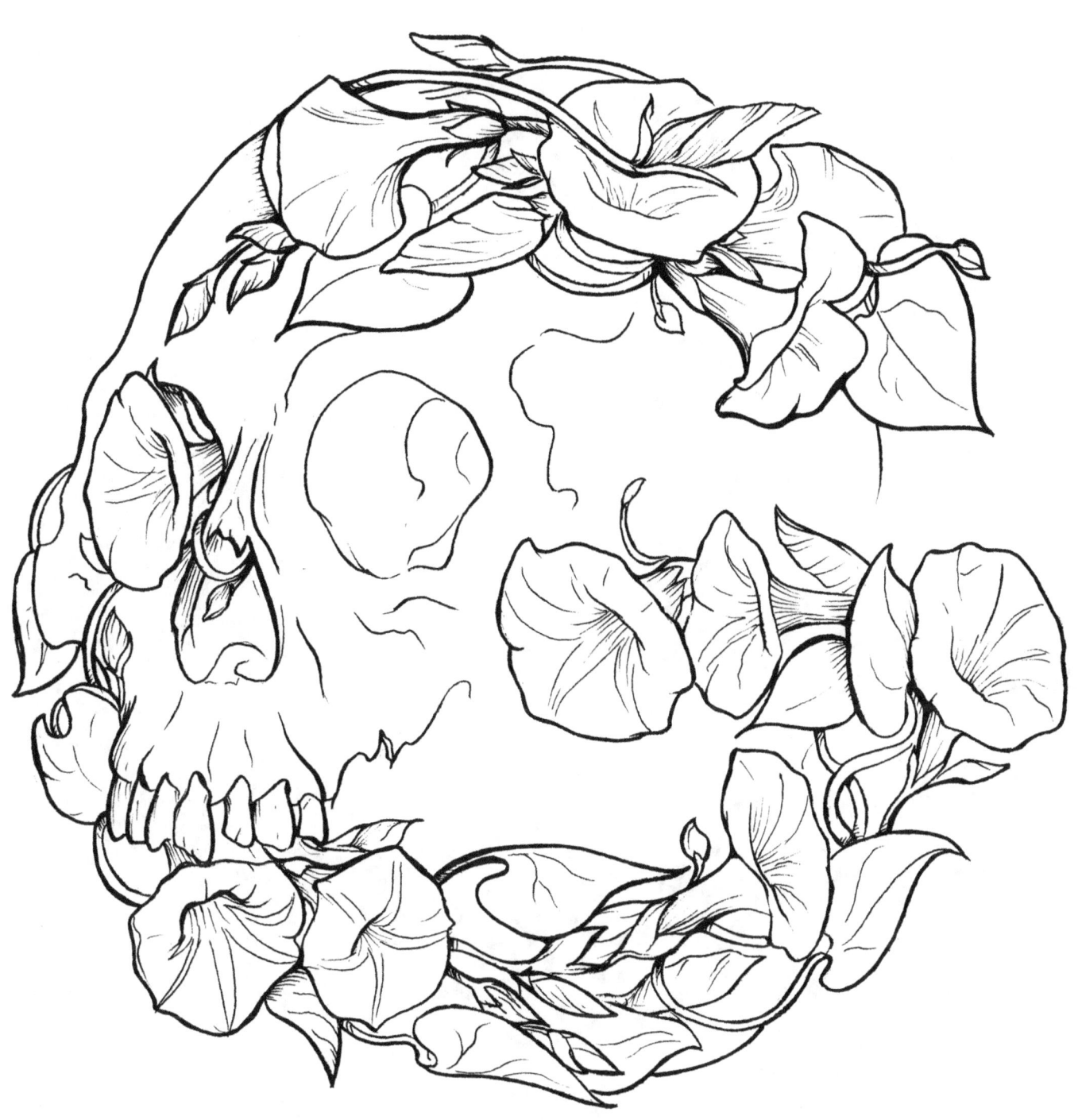

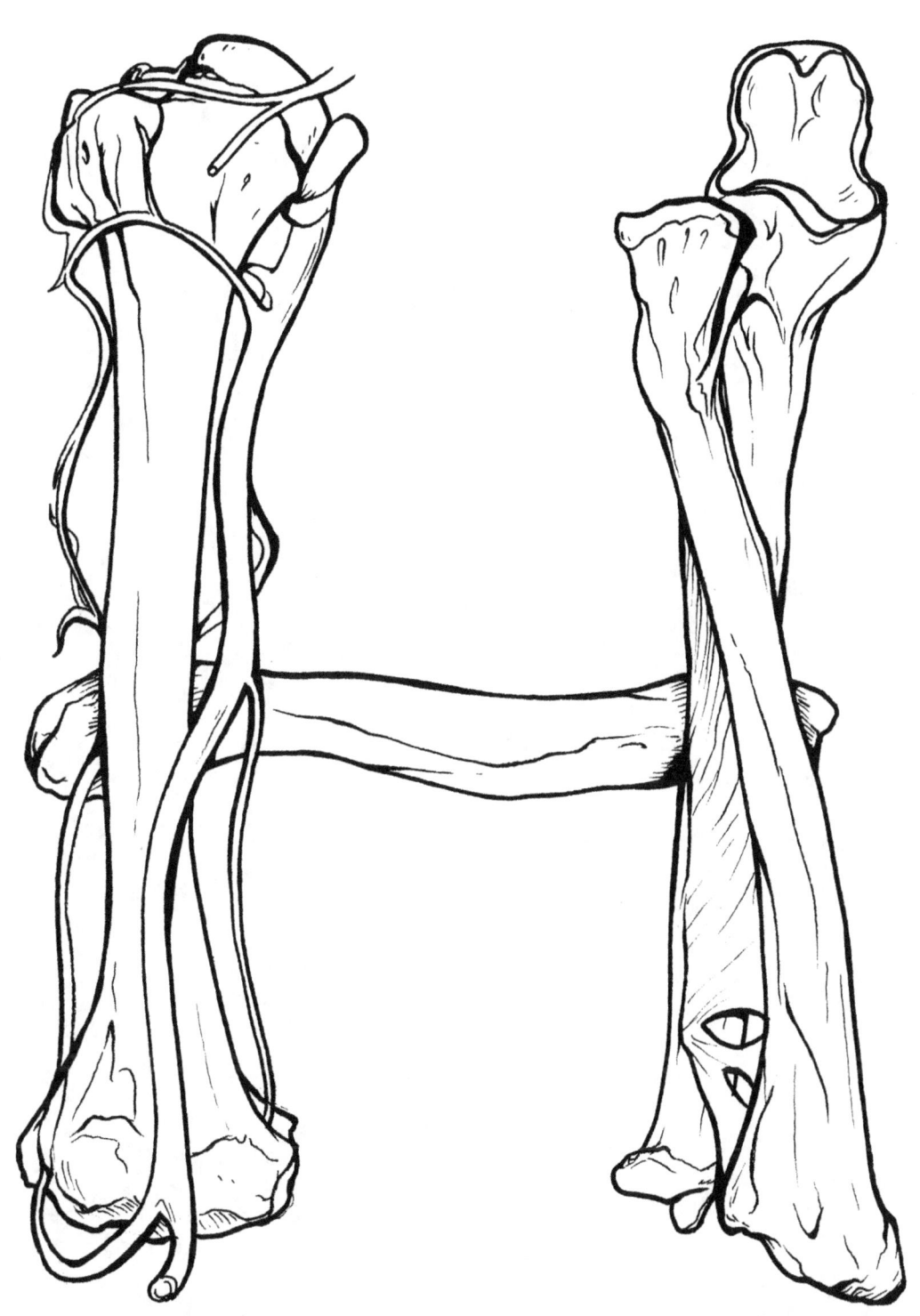

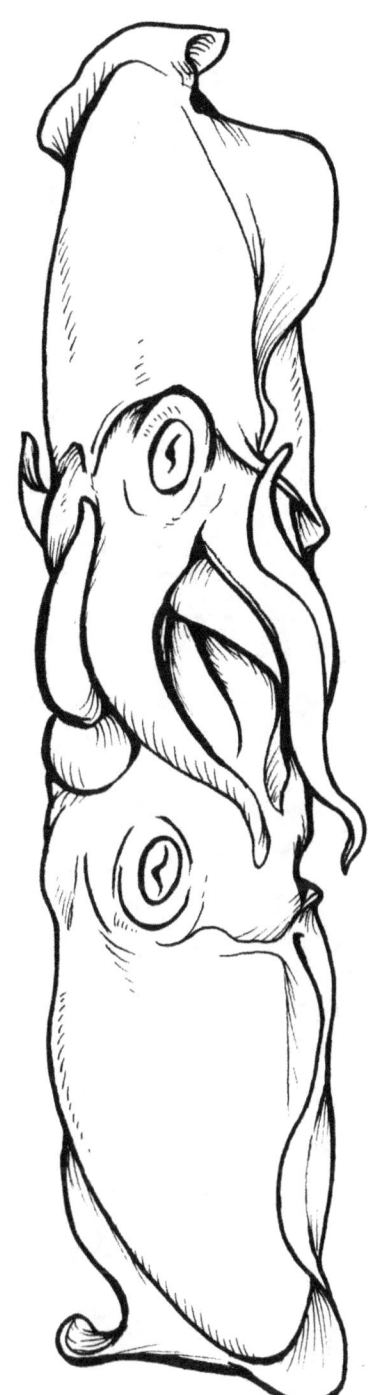

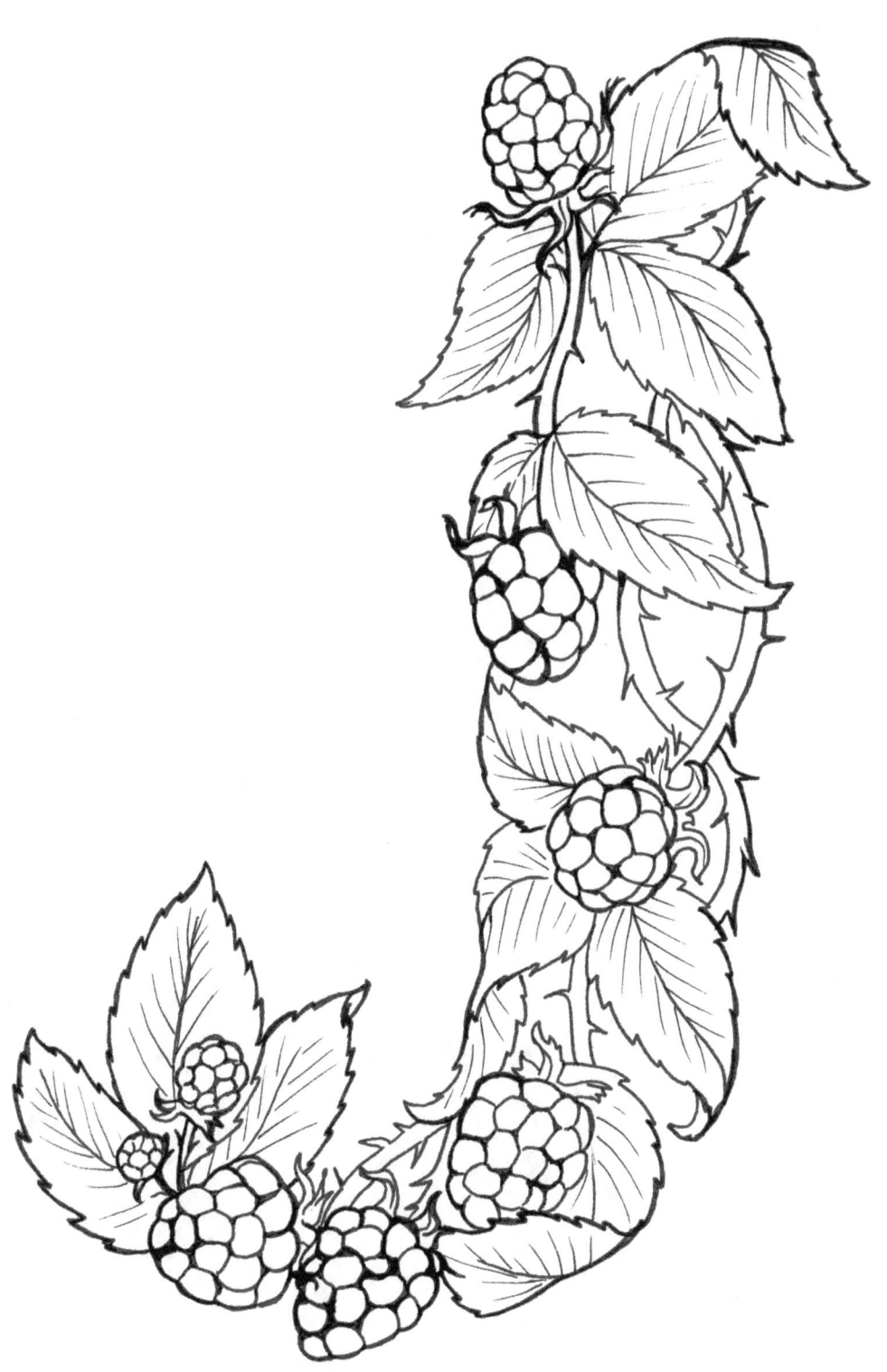

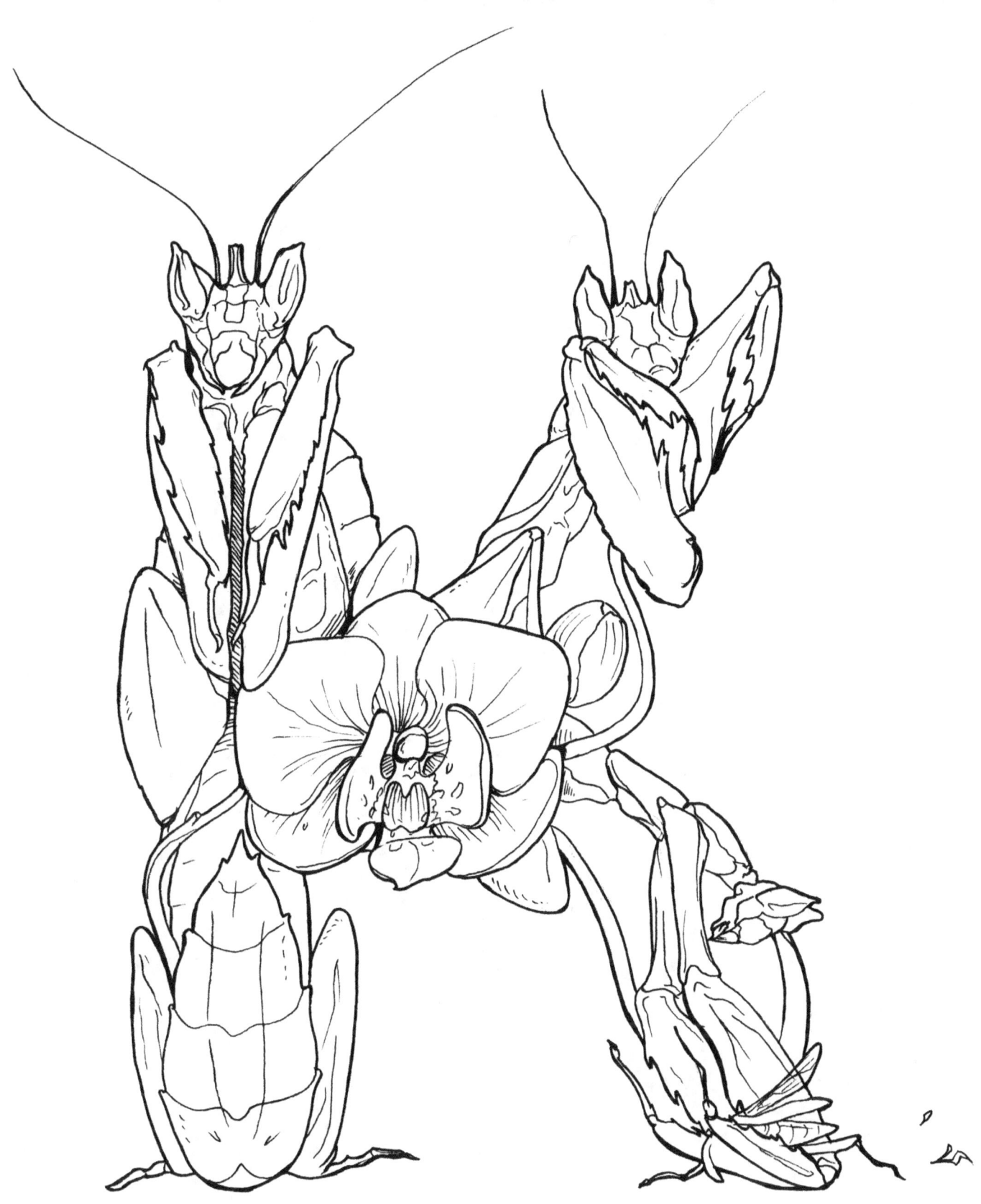

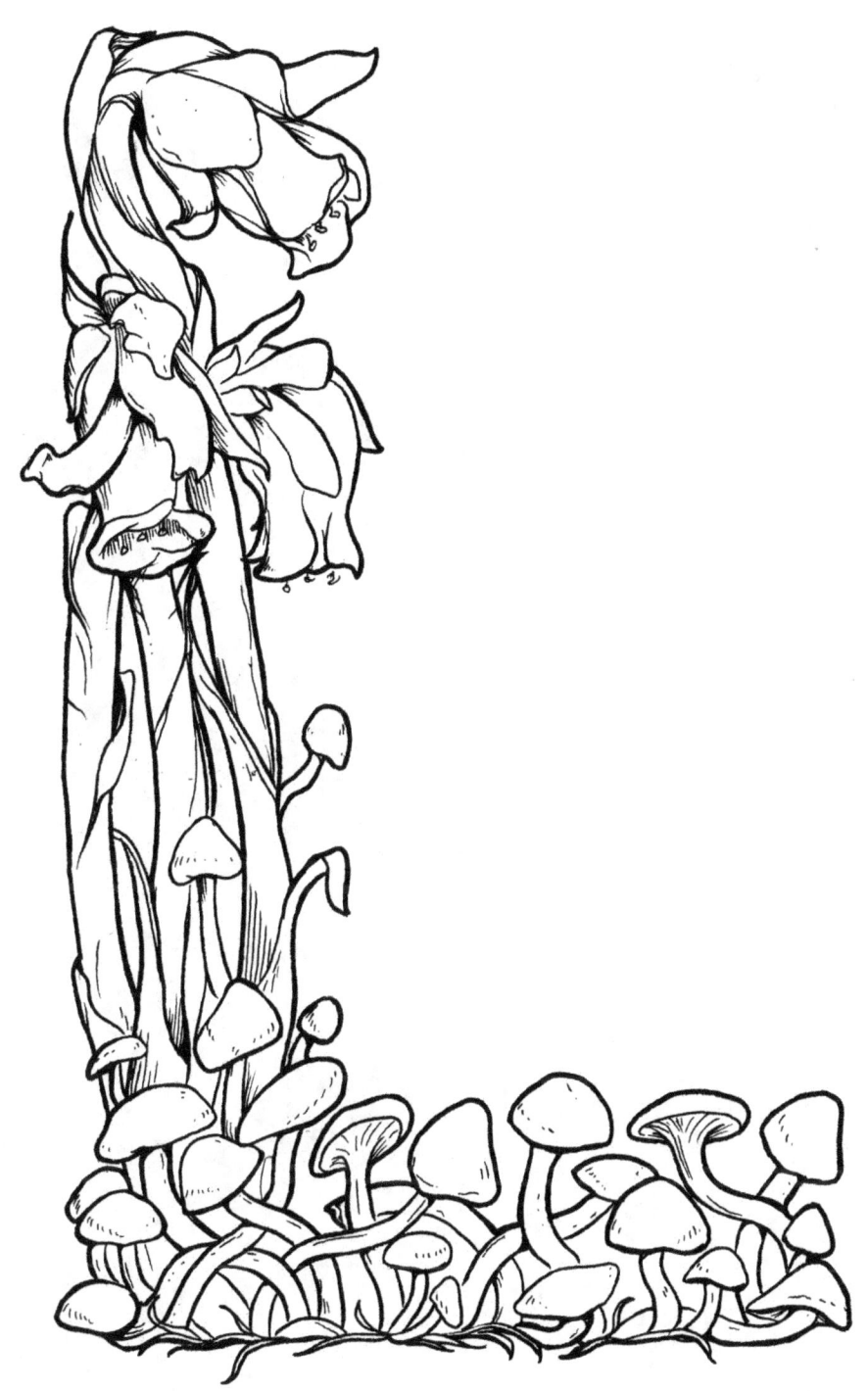

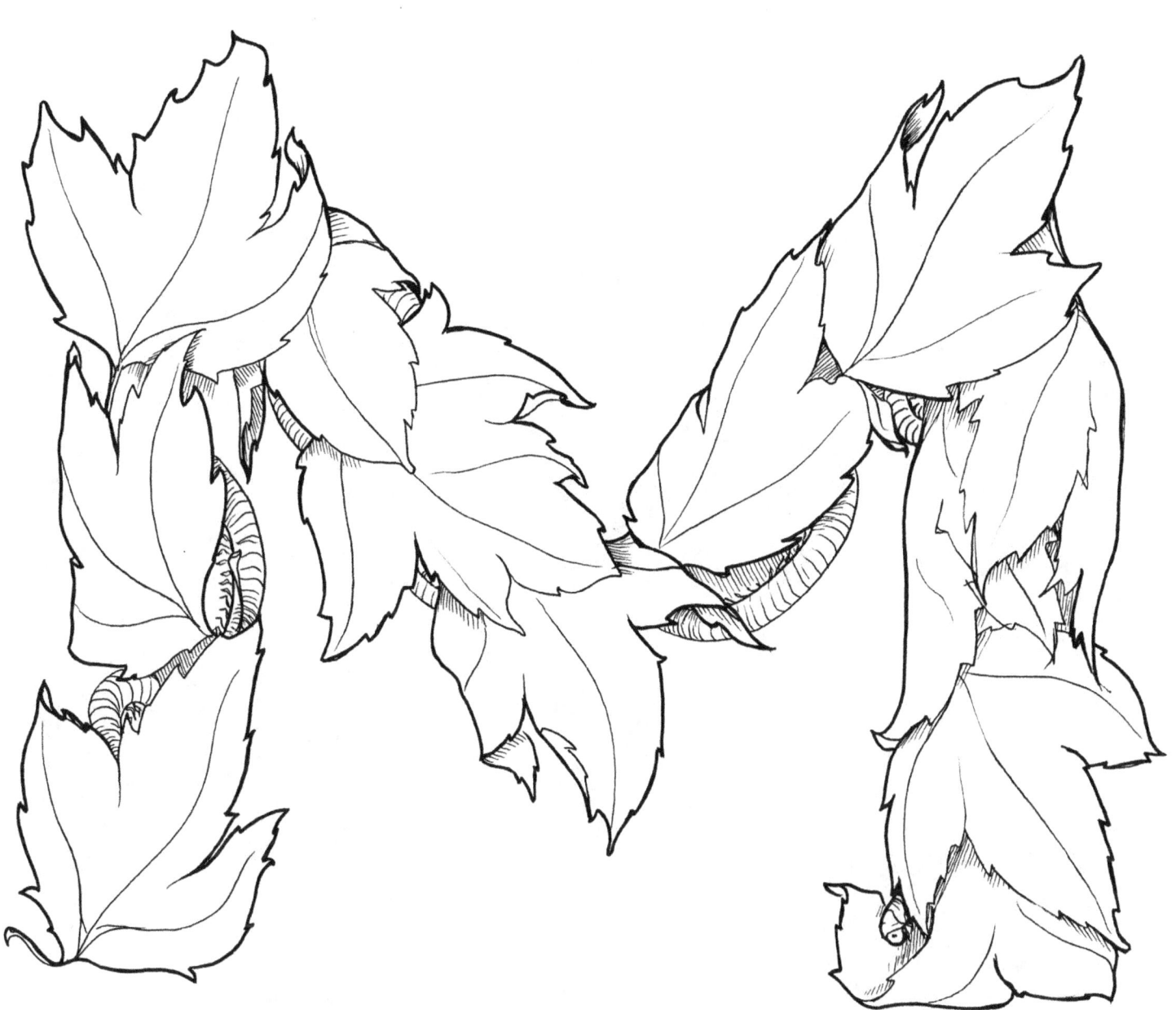

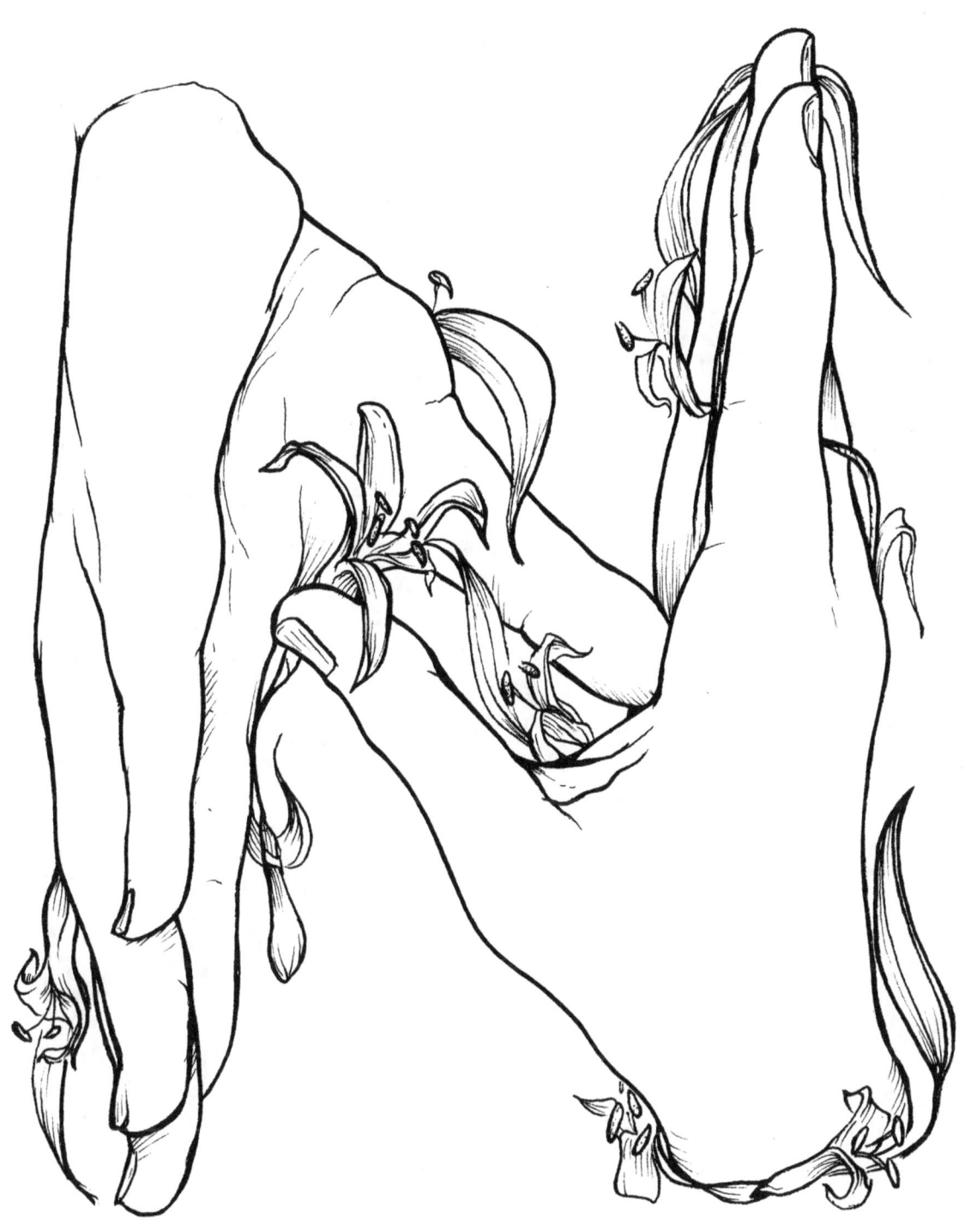

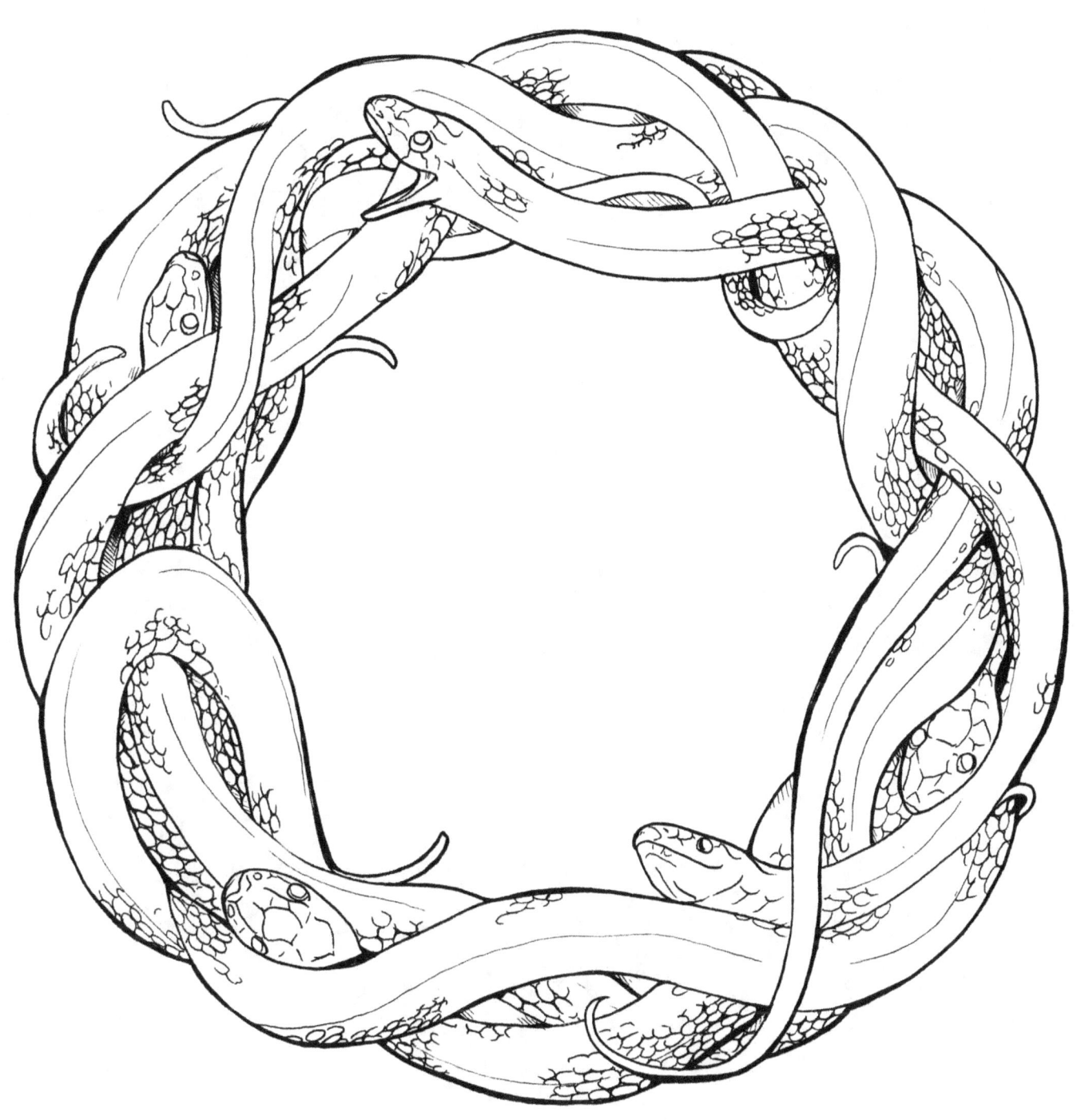

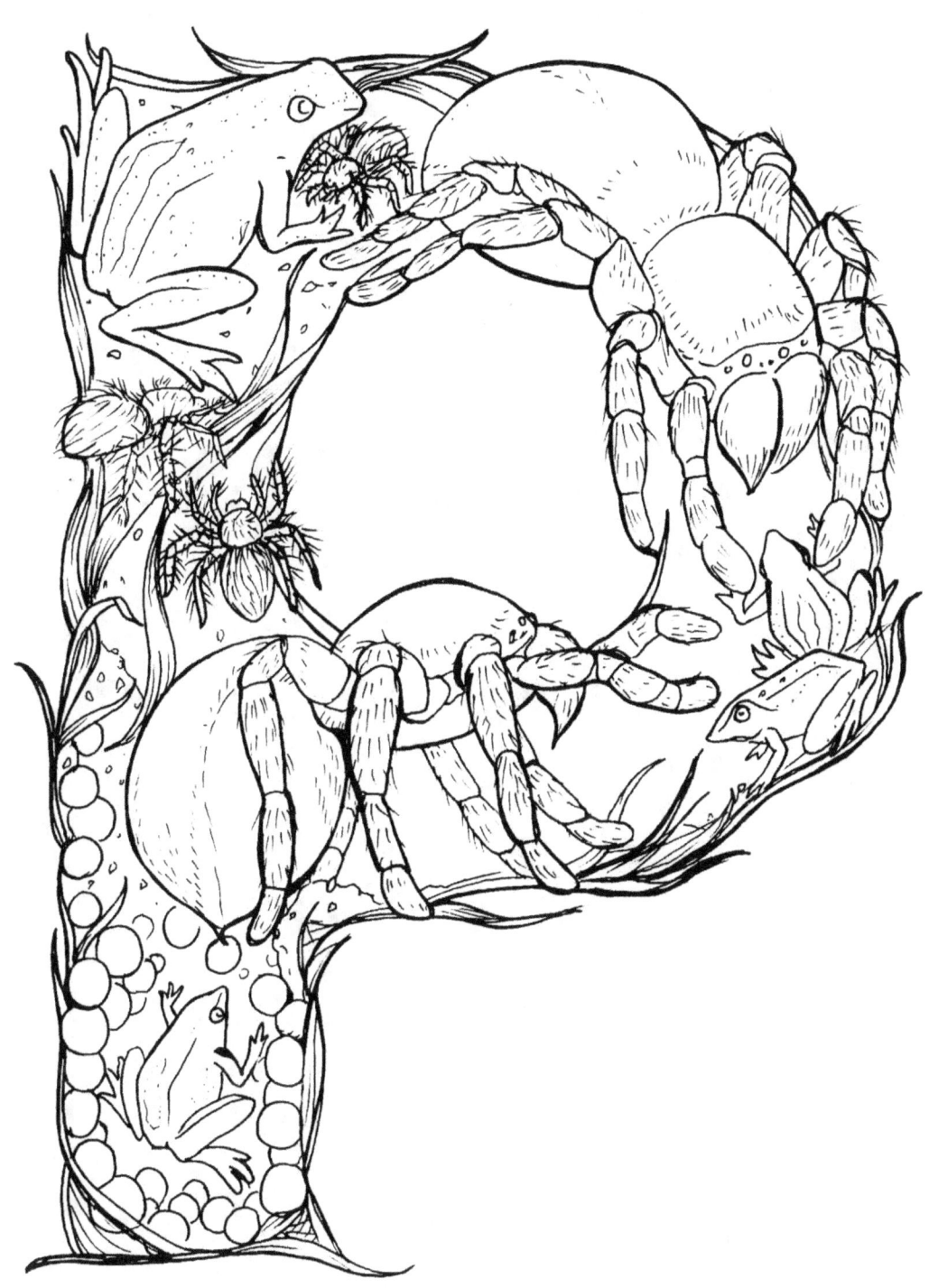

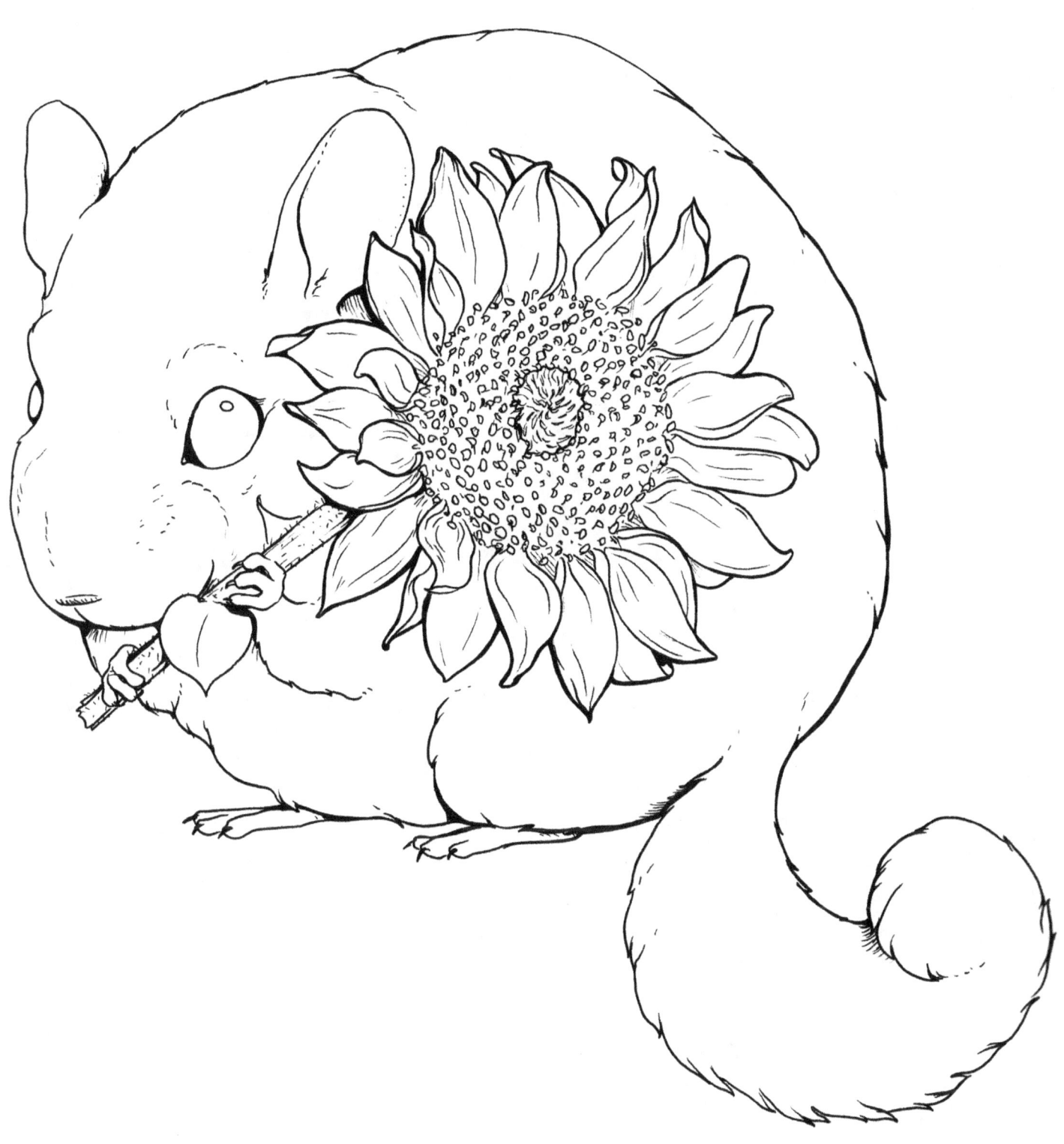

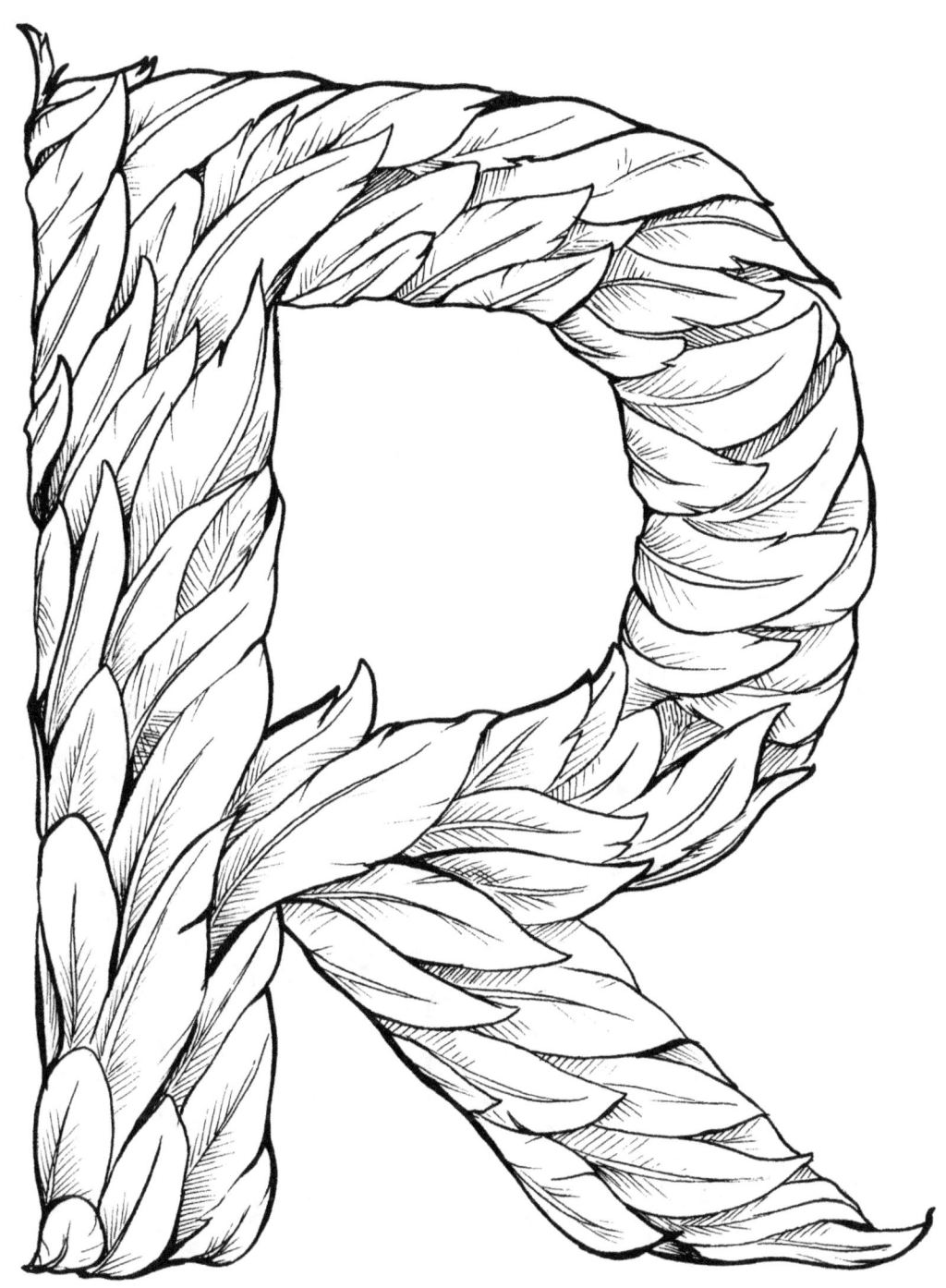

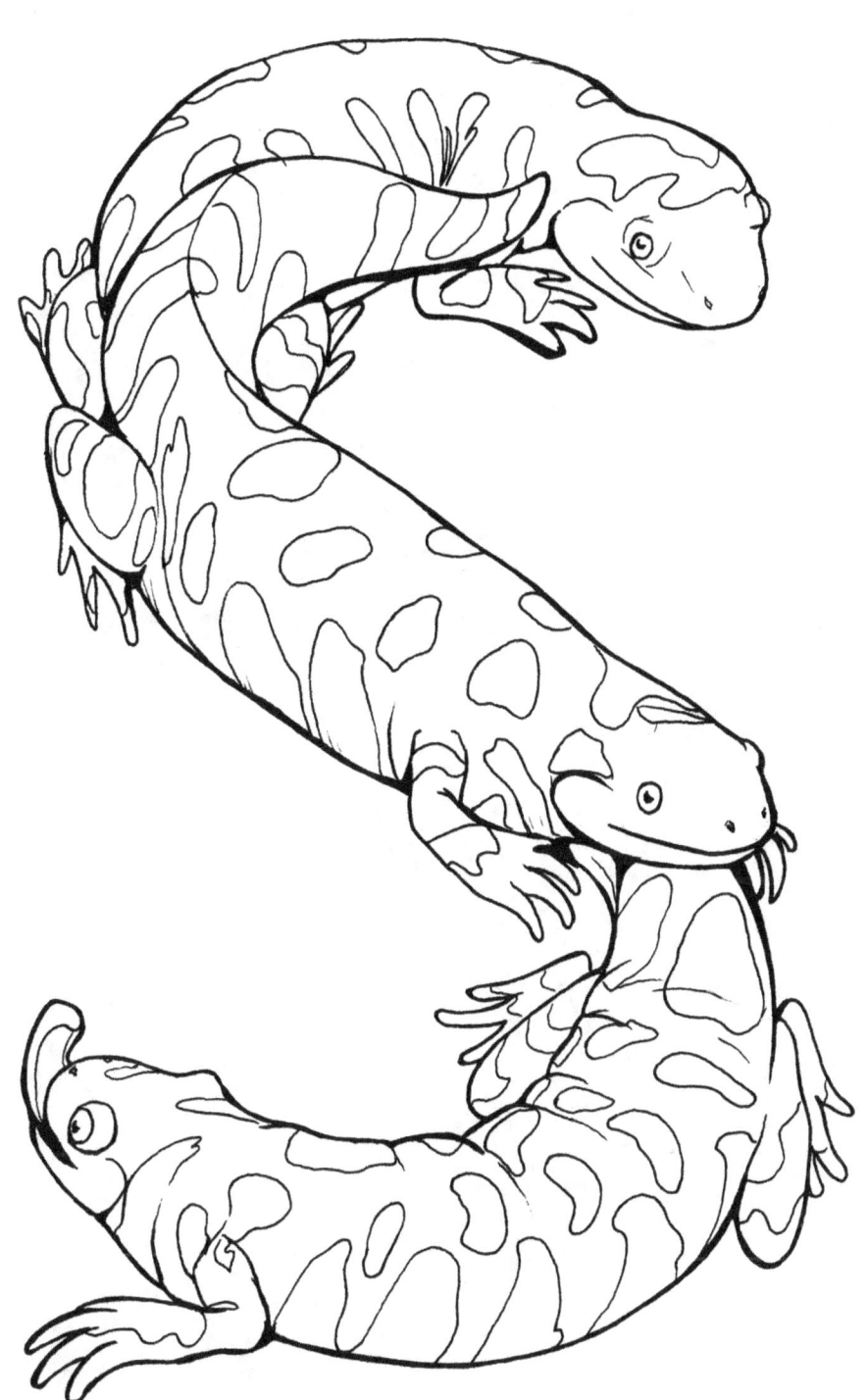

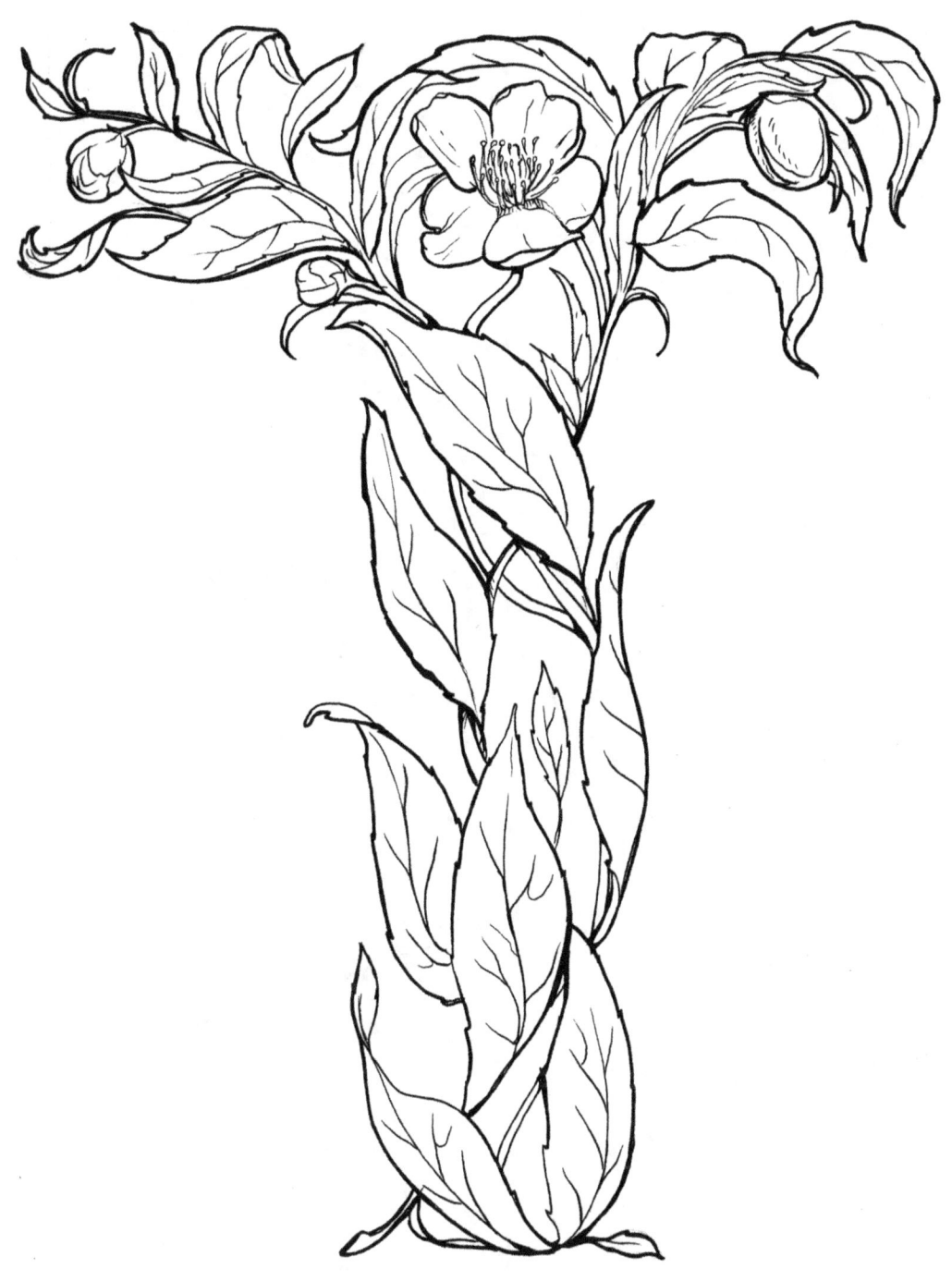

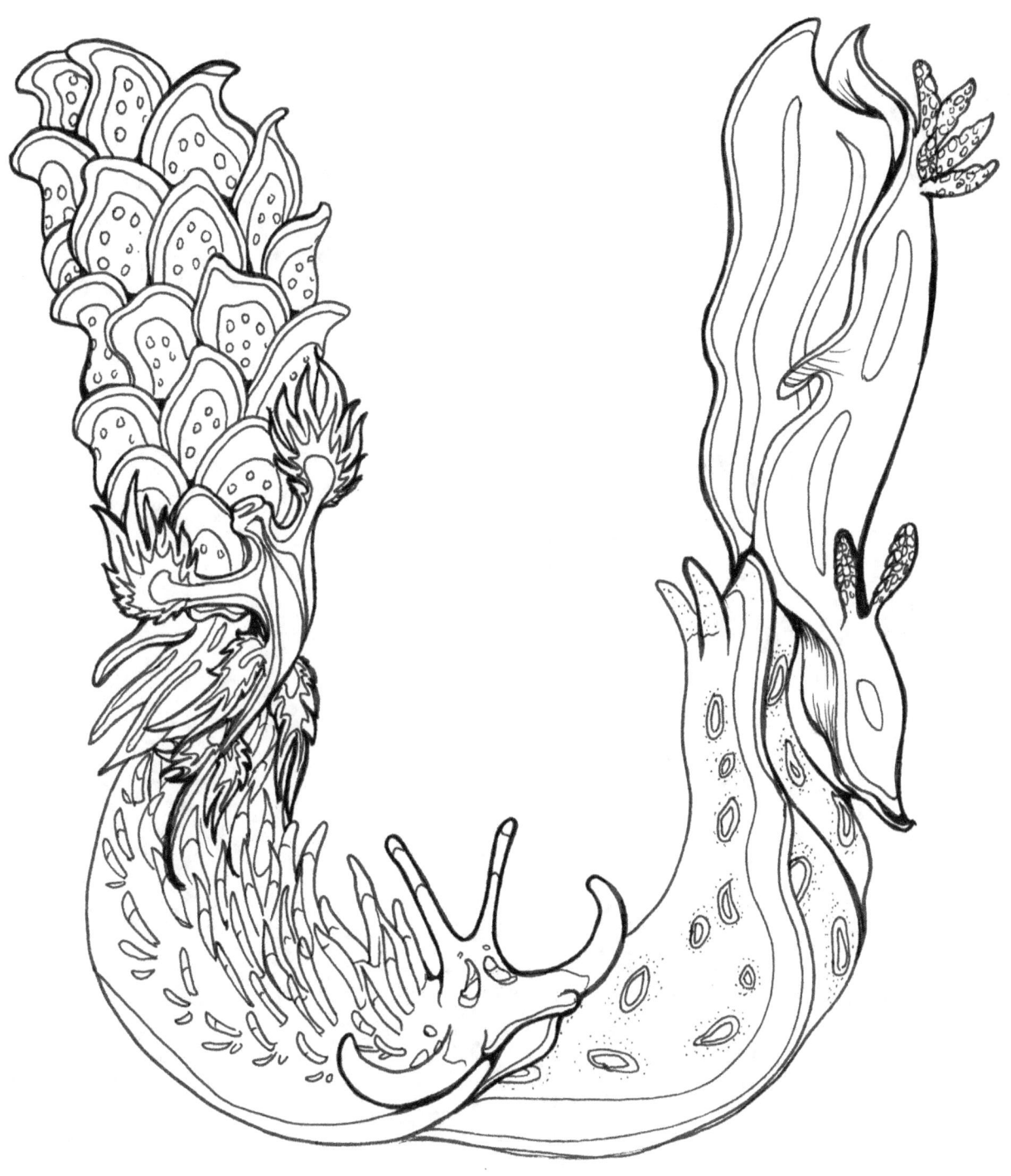

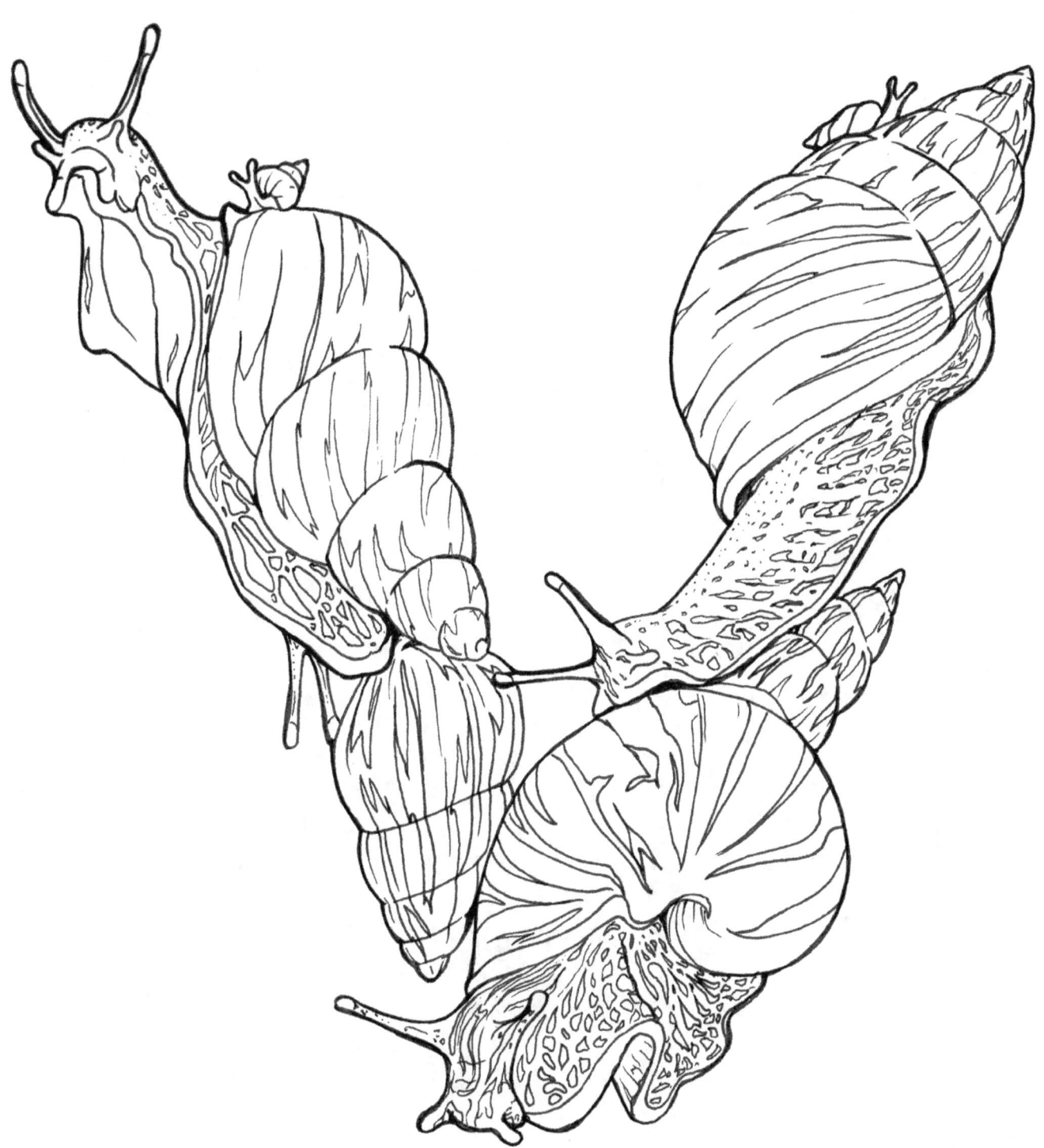

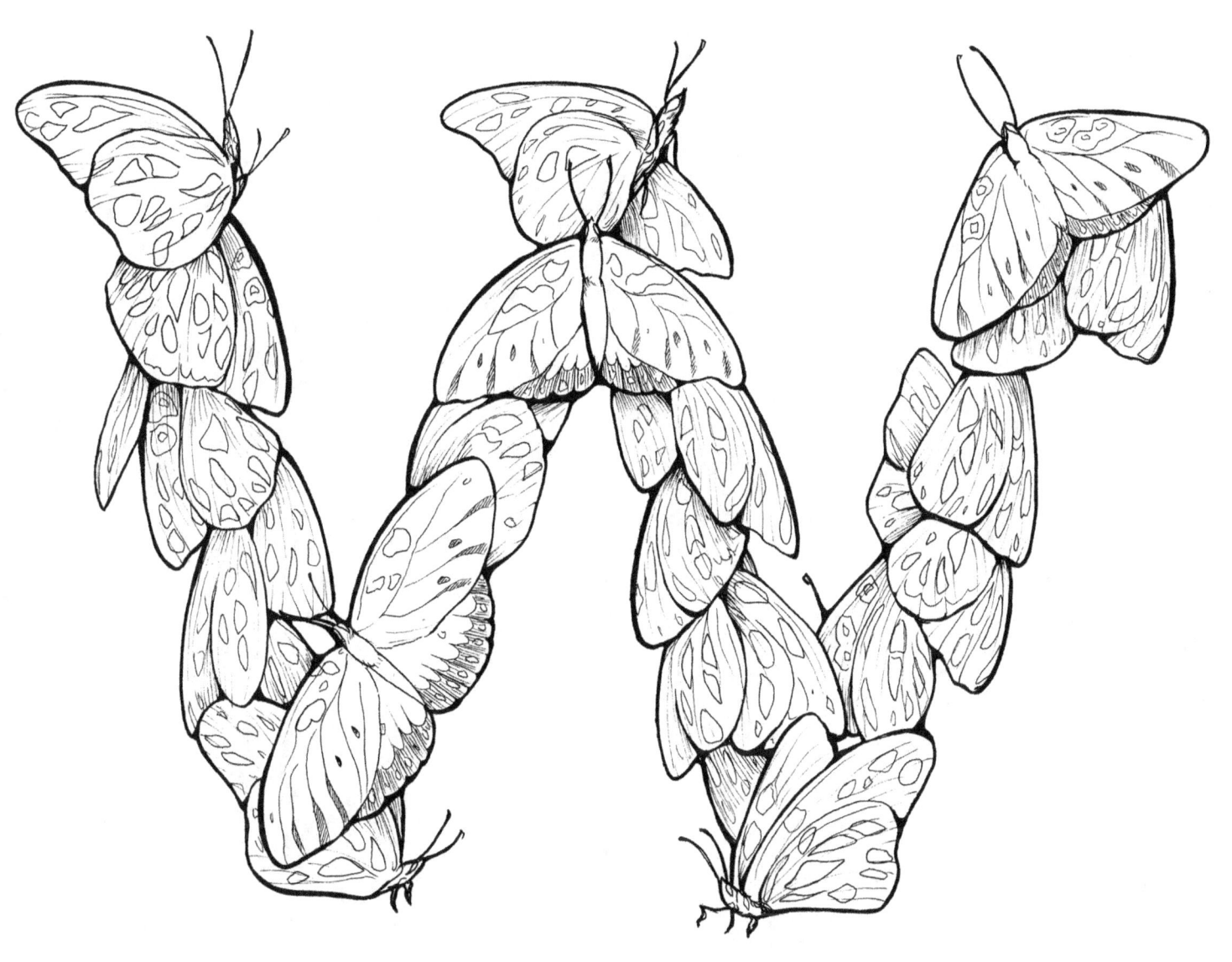

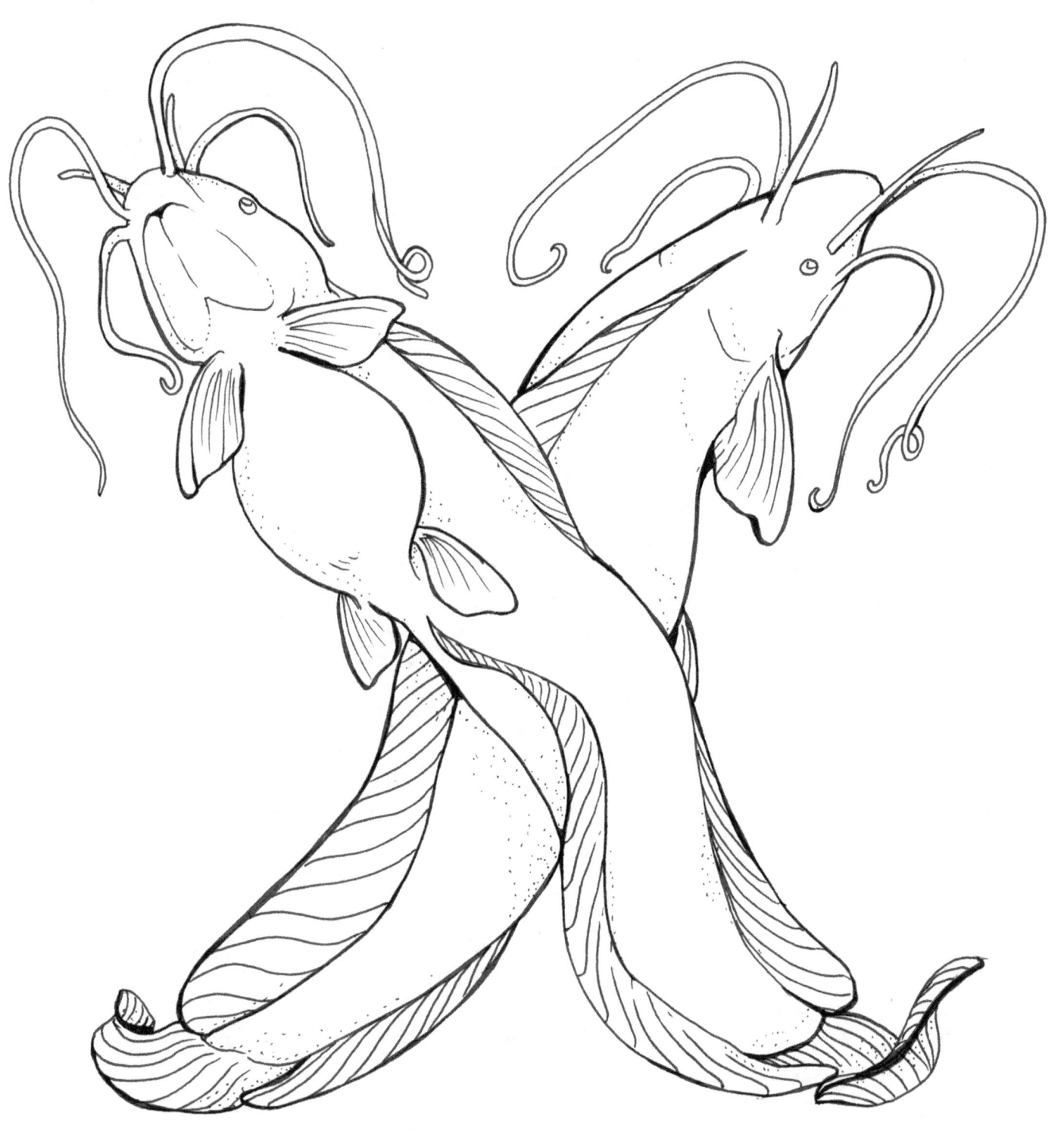

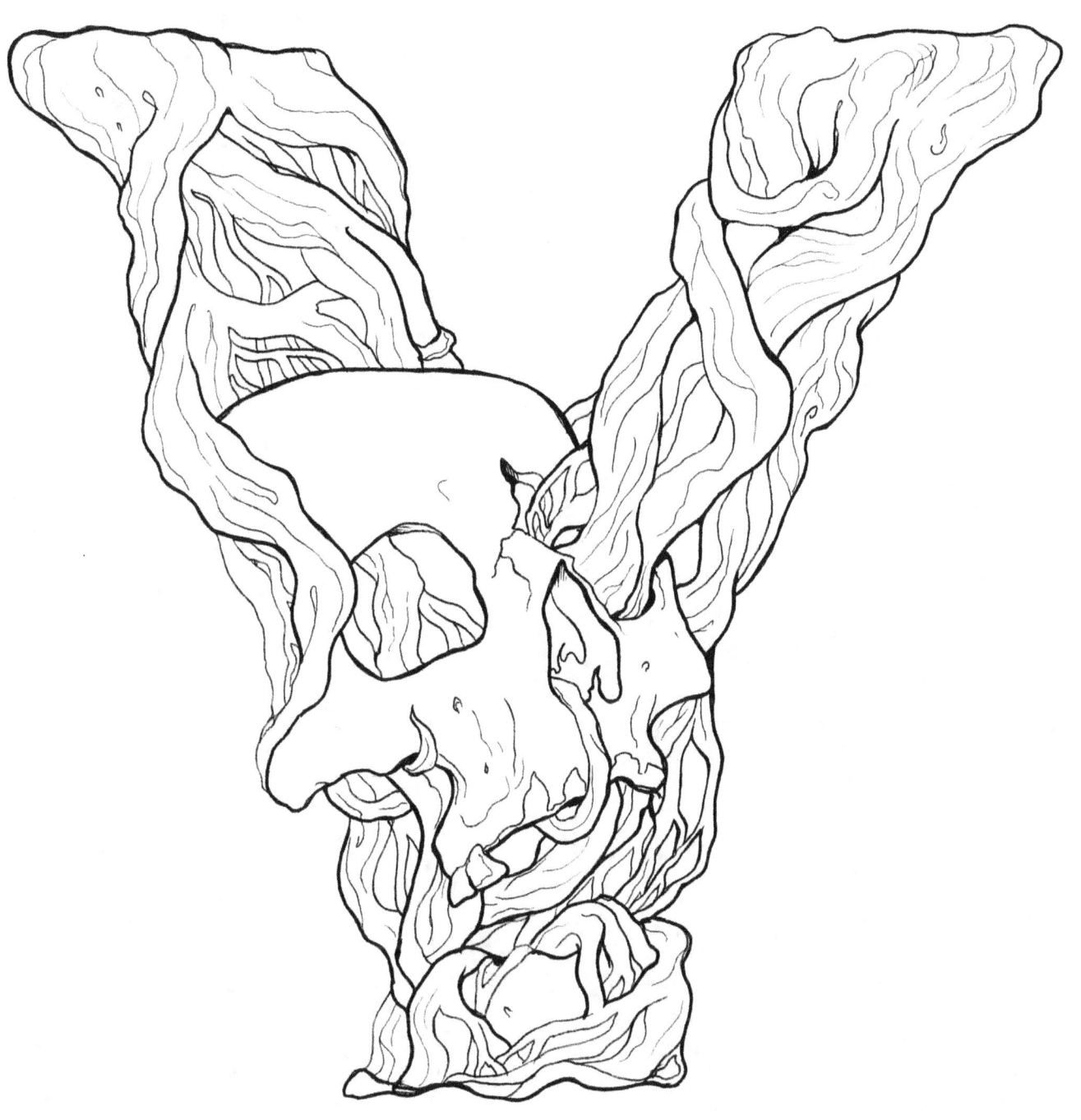

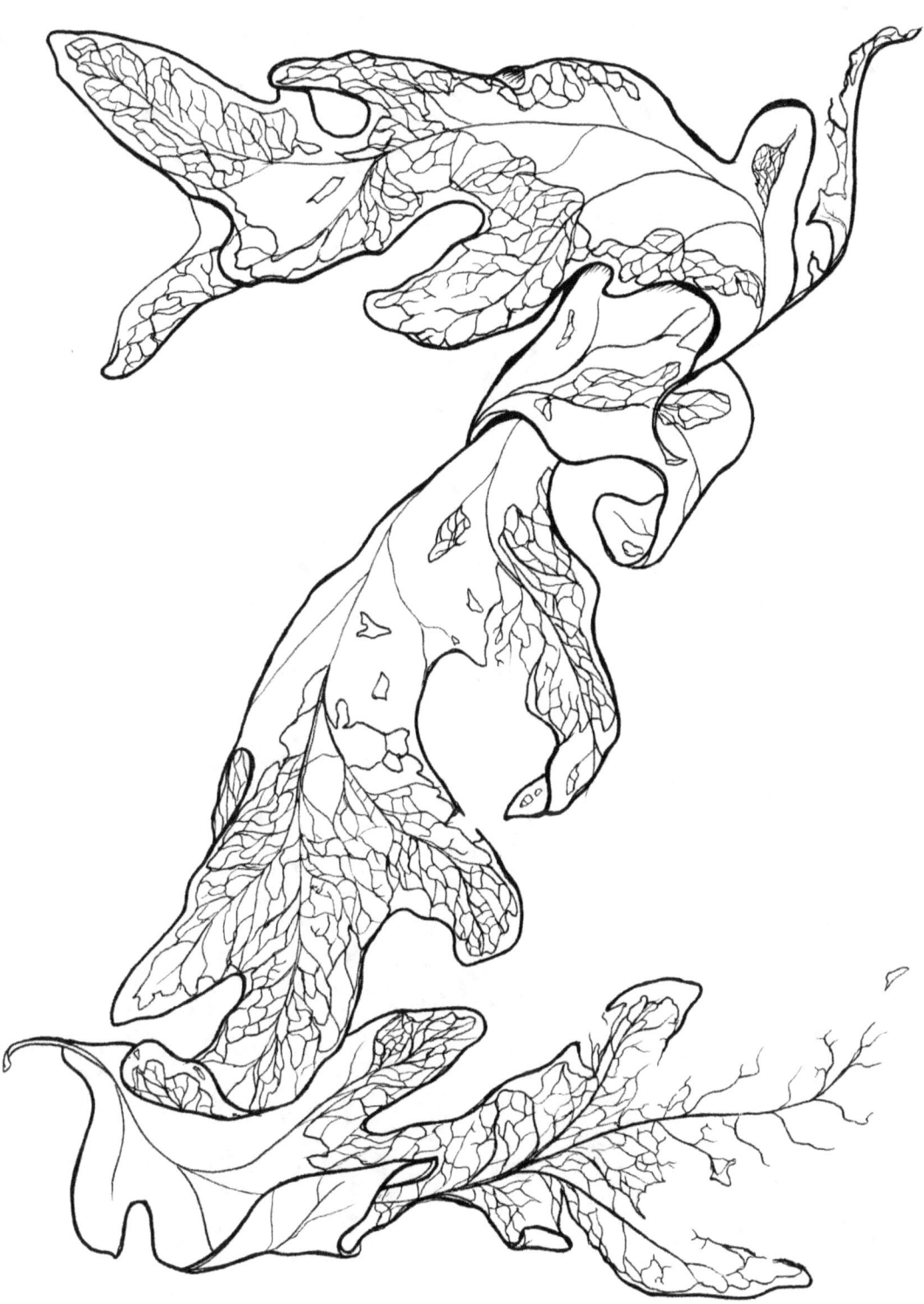

Extras

Thanks to my supporters and fans for making this book possible. In the following pages you'll find an additional letter E and space to draw your own Love Letters.

Feel free to send finished coloring pages and drawings to rheaewing@gmail.com or @finecomic on twitter!

Your Own Love Letter

Your Own Love Letter

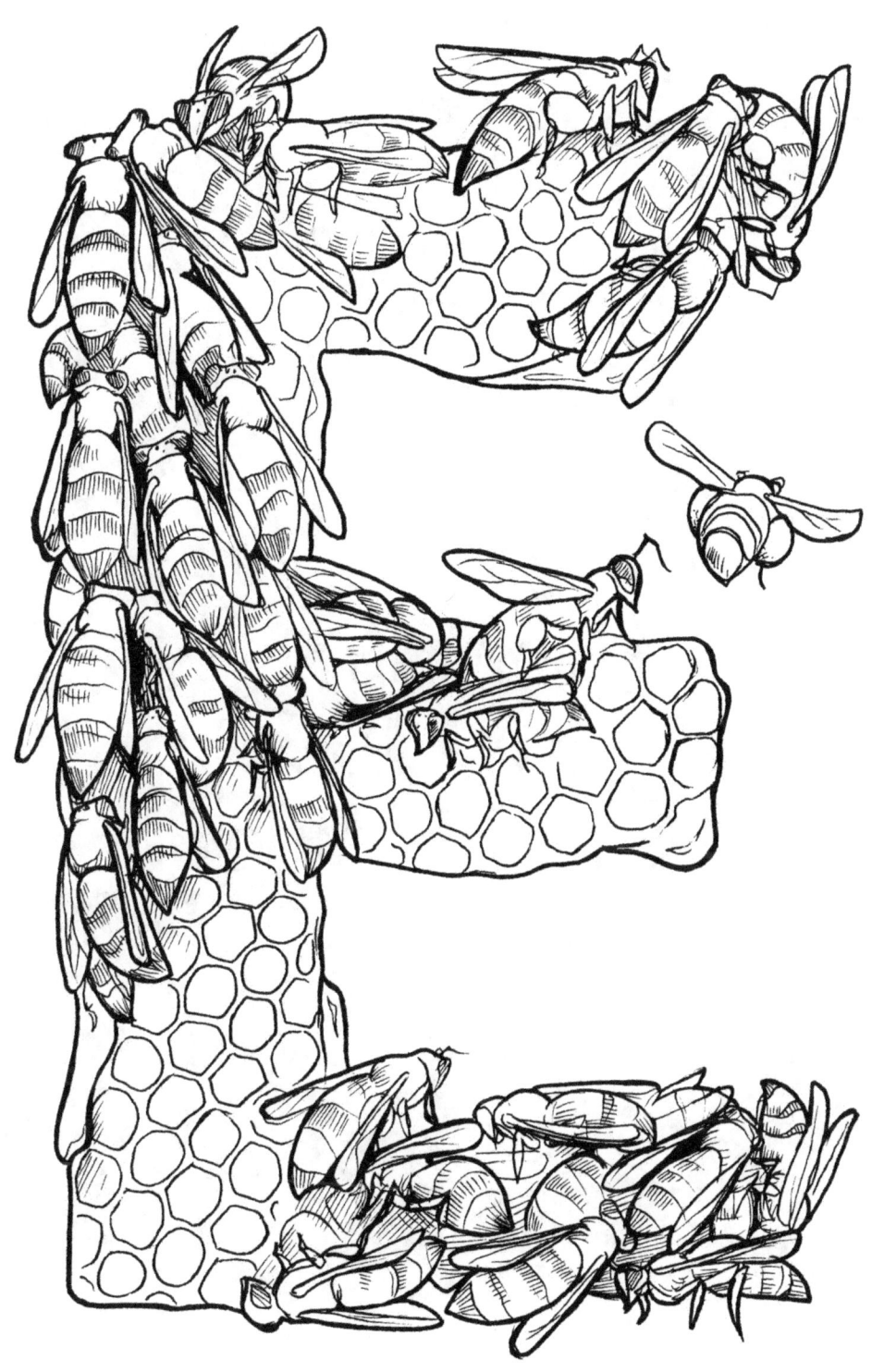

Your Own Love Letter

About the Artist

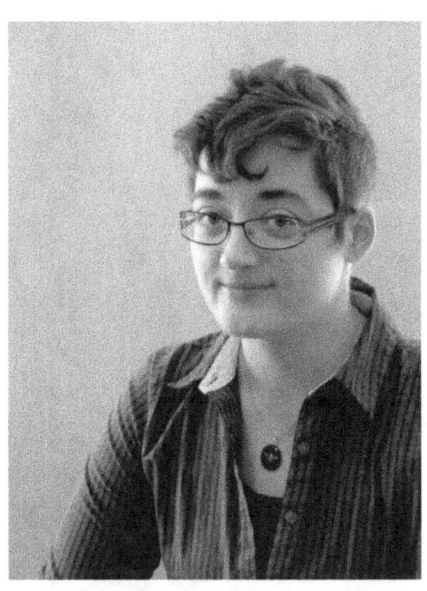

Rhea Ewing is a fine artist and an alumna of UW-Madison. A transplant to the Midwest, Rhea calls Wisconsin "the first place that felt like home" and tries to capture that sense of place in their work.

Rhea also calls upon personal and political themes of living with a queer identity in the Midwest, finding spiritual connections to the natural world, and building safe spaces for all people. The value of art, by their reasoning, is the ability to create connections, question assumptions, and inspire others to do the same.

Rhea currently lives and works in Wisconsin, wandering the hills through frost, fall, and flowers in search of cool bugs and interesting rocks.

In addition to fine art and nature illustrations, Rhea is an avid comic creator. You can see more of their work at rheaewing.com